Contents

Long, long ago, in the town of Nazareth in Galilee, there lived a young woman called Mary. She was engaged to be married to the local carpenter, Joseph. One day, when Mary was busy with her daily chores, the room was filled with light and the angel Gabriel appeared before her. Mary felt very afraid.

"Don't be frightened, Mary," the angel said. "This is a happy day. For God has chosen you to have a baby. A very special baby who will become the saviour of the world. And his name will be Jesus."

"I will do as God wishes," Mary said, bowing her head.

When she looked up, the angel had gone. Later he visited Joseph to bless his marriage to Mary.

Soon afterwards, Mary and Joseph were married. They settled down in Nazareth to look forward to the baby's birth. But their happy life did not last for long. Some months later, the emperor ordered everyone to return to the town of their birth to be counted and taxed. Joseph was born in Bethlehem, a town far away, and he and Mary had to go back there.

It was a long and tiring journey. Mary rode on a donkey while Joseph walked in front. At night they slept by the roadside. And when at last they reached Bethlehem, the town was crowded with travellers like them.

Joseph knew that the baby would soon be born and he anxiously went from door to door, looking for somewhere for them to stay. But everywhere was full. A kindly innkeeper took pity on them.

"I don't have a room to spare," he said. "But you're welcome to sleep in my stable."

And, later that night, in the snug little stable, Mary had her baby. She called him Jesus, as the angel had told her. She wrapped him up warmly and laid him in a manger on a bed of soft hay. The manger was where the animals usually had their food but there was nowhere else for the baby to sleep.

Meanwhile, on a hillside outside the town, a group of shepherds were watching over their sheep. It was late at night and some of the shepherds were dozing off to sleep. Suddenly the sky was filled with dazzling light. The shepherds were terrified and dared not look. When they finally opened their eyes and looked, an angel stood before them.

"I bring you
wonderful news," the angel
said. "Today a baby has been born
in Bethlehem who will be the
saviour of the world. Go
quickly and visit him.
You will find him lying in a manger."
Then the sky was filled with
angels, singing:
"Glory to God in the highest,
And on Earth peace,
Good will to all people."

As soon as the angels had gone, the shepherds hurried to Bethlehem to see Jesus. They found him in the stable, as the angel had promised, and knelt down quietly to worship him. Then they returned to their fields. On the way, they told everyone they met about the amazing things they had seen and heard.

News of Jesus's birth spread far and wide throughout the country. A group of wise men travelled from the east to Jerusalem to look for the baby. A few nights earlier, they had seen a bright star in the sky, a sign that a new king had been born, as the ancient scriptures had said. Now they wanted to worship him.

But when King Herod, the ruler of Jerusalem, heard their story, he was furious. He did not want a rival for his power. So he summoned the wise men to him.

"Once you have found the baby, return to me," he told them. "So that I can worship him too."

But wicked Herod did not want to worship Jesus. He was really plotting to kill him.

The three wise men left Jerusalem and
followed the star to Bethlehem. There they found
Mary, Joseph and the baby Jesus. With great joy,
they knelt down and worshipped him, and gave
him their gifts of precious gold, frankincense and
myrrh. Gifts that were fit for a king.

That night, each of the wise men had the same dream. An angel warned them not to return to Jerusalem but to go home by a different route. Then Herod would not be able to find them.

Soon after the wise
men left, Joseph saw
an angel in his dreams.

"Take Mary and Jesus and
go to Egypt," the angel said.
"Go quickly, there is no time to
lose. Herod is looking for the baby
and if he finds him, he will kill
him for sure."

Joseph woke Mary, and they crept
out of the house, taking Jesus with them.

Their journey to Egypt took many days but at last they reached safety. And there they stayed until an angel visited Joseph again, this time with good news. Herod was dead, and, at last, Mary, Joseph and Jesus were able to go home to Nazareth.

Christmas Celebrations

Each year, Christians all over the world celebrate Jesus's birth with church services, gifts, cards and special food. No one knows exactly when Jesus was born. Christians chose 25 December because this was the date of a Roman winter festival. Many Christians in the Eastern Orthodox churches celebrate Christmas on 7 January.

Angels from Heaven

Angels play an important part in Bible stories. They are believed to be heavenly beings who carry messages and prayers between Heaven and Earth. The archangel Gabriel (seen in the picture below) is one of the angels who bring messages from God to people on Earth. It is he who announces the birth of Jesus to Mary. Angels are often pictured as beautiful, shining beings, flying on wings and with haloes around their heads. Their beauty is a sign of God's glory.

Away in a Manger

A-way in a man-ger no crib for a bed, The

lit — tle Lord Je-sus laid down His sweet head. The

stars in the bright sky looked down where He lay, The

lit — tle Lord Je - sus a - sleep on the hay.

The cattle are lowing, the Baby awakes,
But little Lord Jesus no crying He makes.
I love Thee, Lord Jesus! Look down from the sky,
And stay by my side until morning is nigh.

Be near me, Lord Jesus; I ask Thee to stay
Close by me for ever, and love me, I pray.
Bless all the dear children in Thy tender care,
And fit us for heaven, to live with Thee there.

A Christmas Recipe

ALWAYS ASK AN ADULT TO HELP YOU

Christmas Biscuits

Ingredients:
100g softened butter
50g caster sugar
175g plain flour
A pinch of salt
A few drops of vanilla essence

Decoration:
Tubes of coloured writing icing
Coloured sugar balls

What to do:
1. Ask an adult to pre-heat the oven to 180°C/ 350°F/ Gas Mark 4 for you.
2. Beat the butter and sugar together with a wooden spoon.
3. Add a few drops of vanilla essence.
4. Sift in the flour and salt, bit by bit, and stir until you have a stiff dough. If the dough is too dry, add a little water.
5. Make the dough into a ball using your hands and then roll it out on a floured surface, using a rolling pin dusted with flour.
6. Cut into Christmas shapes (such as stars and Christmas trees) using biscuit cutters.
7. Place the biscuits on a greased baking tray and ask an adult to put them in the oven for you.
8. Bake them for 15 minutes or until they are golden brown.
9. Leave the biscuits to cool for a while and then use the writing icing and sugar balls to decorate them.